ACHIEVING HIGH
PERFORMANCE

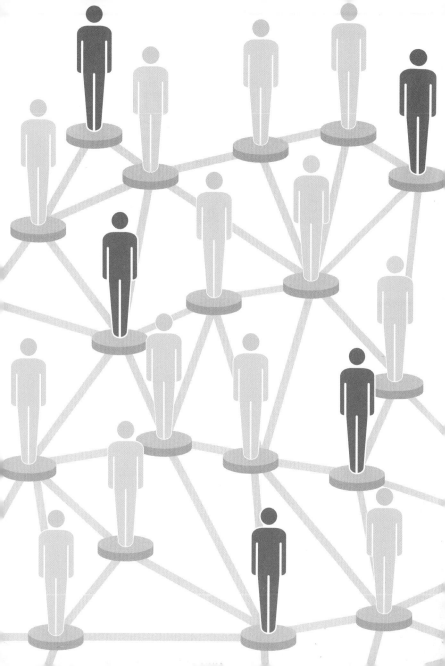

ESSENTIAL MANAGERS

ACHIEVING HIGH PERFORMANCE

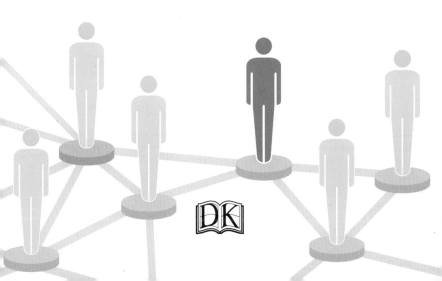

DK

Written by Mike Bourne and Pippa Bourne

Senior Art Editor Gillian Andrews
Project Editor Hugo Wilkinson
Designer XAB Design
Editor Louise Tucker
US Editors Margaret Parrish, Jill Hamilton
Managing Editor Gareth Jones
Senior Managing Art Editor Lee Griffiths
Production Editor Nikoleta Parasaki
Production Controller Mandy Inness
Jacket Designer Mark Cavanagh
Design Development Manager Sophia M.T.T.

Delhi Team:
Senior Editorial Manager Rohan Sinha
Deputy Managing Art Editor Sudakshina Basu

First published in 2009 by
Dorling Kindersley Limited
80 Strand
London WC2R 0RL
A Penguin Random House Company

15 16 17 18 10 9 8 7 6 5 4 3 2 1

001-279387-May/2015

A CIP catalogue record for this book is
available from the British Library.

ISBN 978-0-2411-8614-5

Colour reproduction by
Colourscan, Singapore
Printed in China

www.dk.com

Contents

Introduction

There is no single technique for achieving excellence at work. High performance is attained through a combination of understanding yourself and your strengths and limitations; knowing what you want to achieve; and ensuring you are in an environment where you enjoy working and have some freedom to achieve what you want. **Achieving High Performance** gives you the tools you need to address these areas, and so become more successful at what you do.

Your route to improvement starts by getting to know yourself. The more fully you understand yourself, the more confident you will be. By understanding and playing to your strengths, you have a better chance of succeeding at your endeavours. Of course, you need to develop skills and knowledge in your chosen field. There are some skills, such as managing your time and presenting, that will apply whatever you are doing and wherever you are doing it. These are like the tools in your work box, and the key to acquiring and honing them is to practise.

To become more effective at work, you need to be creative and confident, to communicate and listen well, and to make difficult decisions. If you can master these sometimes intangible skills, you can really differentiate yourself from other people. Finally, achieving high performance is about developing your skills further into management and leadership, broadening your horizons, and making use of what other people have to offer you.

Knowing
yourself

To prosper in both life and business you need to understand yourself. What are your strengths and limitations, what do you enjoy, and what do you really want to achieve? By reflecting upon and analyzing your own characteristics, and how you are perceived by others, you can begin to produce a plan for self-development and ultimate success.

01

Looking in from outside

Other people's perceptions of you may be significantly at odds with your own view of yourself. Finding out what others think of you is an important element of self-exploration, and helps you modify your behaviour so that you can take up opportunities that you might otherwise have missed.

Seeking new perspectives

You may feel you lack confidence, or that you are too quiet, but others may see you primarily as someone who is trustworthy, honourable, and wise. Conversely, you may describe yourself as assertive and confident, while others see you as aggressive and avoid involving you in their projects. Other people's views are important because they shape the way they behave towards you. That's not to say you should always aim to please others, or change the person you are, but being aware of how others see you will enable you to change the signals you send out.

33%

of **employers** in one survey said they took only **90 seconds** to decide to hire a person

In focus

PSYCHOMETRIC TESTING

Psychometric tests, such as the widely used Myers Briggs, offer a psychological approach to self-understanding. These tests look at personality and attempt to give an indication of the type of environment in which an individual is likely to thrive. Myers-Briggs Type Indicator positions people against four pairs of factors:
• Extroversion and introversion
• Sensing and intuition
• Thinking and feeling
• Judging and perceiving
There is nothing wrong with any of these personality traits. However, if, for example, you are at the extreme end of the scale on "thinking", you may be ignoring people's feelings when you make decisions. If you are a "perceiving" rather than a "judging" person, you may need to set more goals and deadlines for yourself.

Getting answers

The only way to find out what other people think of you is to ask. Many international companies use a process called 360-degree feedback, which is a formal means of eliciting comment from colleagues, staff, and bosses. It is often used to develop senior management teams, but you can carry out a similar process yourself on a smaller scale.

Approach people who see you in different roles – perhaps your business partner, work colleagues at the same level of management, your immediate boss, some of your suppliers and clients, and a couple of friends. Think of the best way to ask the questions: a questionnaire has the advantage of ensuring consistency, while structured, face-to-face interviews give respondents the opportunity to elaborate, but may also inhibit honest responses. When you are drafting a questionnaire, keep it short and simple, and concentrate on specific questions that you really want answered, such as:

- How confident do I appear to you?
- Am I approachable?
- Do I communicate clearly?

Tip

MAKE AN IMPRESSION
Lasting judgements can be made, based on subconscious cues, within the **first few seconds** of meeting. Think about any **visual cues** you display and the **tone of voice** you use – these can often be **more significant** than what you actually say.

Using feedback

The feedback process won't give you a definitive view of what you are like in the eyes of others, but it is certain to produce some valuable insights. It's too easy to focus on criticisms when you see them in black and white, so make sure that you value and reflect on the positive points that emerge, and use them in your planning for the future.

Setting goals

Work takes up a large chunk of your life, so job satisfaction is important. Achieving it doesn't necessarily mean changing job, it could just be a matter of broadening your existing role. Knowing what you enjoy and want to achieve will help ensure you're in the right job. If you're in the right job, you're more likely to succeed at what you do.

Examining your ambitions

Getting a clear view of your ambitions is not quite as easy as it seems. First, you may have arrived where you are more by chance than by design and it can be hard to avoid being influenced by your current situation. So, if you are working in sales, you may not look beyond a future in which you progress through the ranks to become sales manager and then sales director. Second, you will have family ties or other responsibilities that limit your freedom to follow your dreams. Third, your "ideal" job will change over time as you develop skills and experience.

> Think graphically and generate images of **your ideal world**

Looking at the future

There are many ways to systematically look at your career and life goals. Some people prefer to work with a coach – an objective, sympathetic, and experienced person who can help identify directions for progress. Others favour less formal consultation with their colleagues or peers, but it is equally valid to work through the options on your own. Indeed, the question is so central that it is worth applying more than one approach and repeating the analysis from time to time as your circumstances change.

80%

of people in one survey **admitted** that they lacked **a goal** in life

Visualizing the way

Visualization is a technique that can help you clarify your goals. Set aside some time to sit undisturbed and relaxed. Picture yourself at various points in the future, say in three, five, and ten years' time. Think graphically and generate images of your ideal world, asking yourself questions such as:

- Where will I be living?
- What job will I have?
- What type of organization will I be working in?
- Will I own and be running my own business?
- What will I be doing on a daily basis?
- Will I have a team working for me or will I be a specialist?
- Will I be commuting or working from home, perhaps?
- What will my interests be?

Note down your thoughts and assess the picture that emerges against fixed constraints, such as your obligations to your family.

Now reflect on the results. How can you work towards being where you would like to be? This process is not intended to make you dissatisfied with your present circumstances, but to open your eyes to new possibilities.

Tip

THINK BIG
Reach for the sky – it is important to **dream** before you do a reality check.

How to discover what is important to you

↓

Take five sticky notes.

↓

Write on each sticky note something you currently enjoy at work, for example "managing my team".

↓

Take another five sticky notes in a different colour.

↓

Write on each sticky note something you would like to do, but currently do not, for example "travel".

↓

Arrange all of the sticky notes on the wall in order of priority.

Analyzing your strengths and limitations

To achieve high performance in your workplace, you need to understand and play to your strengths. You also need to recognize what you are less good at doing, so that you can develop appropriate skills and acquire the necessary knowledge and experience.

Describing your capabilities

When you ask yourself what you are really good at, your answer should encompass three important areas – your basic technical ability, your innate personal, or soft, skills, and the knowledge and experience that you have acquired throughout your career.

Most people have a preference for what they like to do. Some people are good at working with numbers, while others excel at languages. These skills are the building blocks of your job – they are sometimes called your basic technical ability.

Tip

REVIEW YOUR SKILLS
Even if you plan to stay in the same job, **look closely** at what's happening around you. Your work environment is in flux and you should **constantly be learning and adapting**, to cope and thrive with the **new circumstances** your workplace presents to you.

Gaining skills and experience

"Soft" skills are less tangible than basic technical ability. You may be a good listener or a powerful communicator, or have the ability to influence people or negotiate well, or you may command respect, have great presence, and be highly motivated. You need to achieve a certain level of skill in all these areas, but that level will depend on your precise role in the organization.

The third dimension of your personal strengths and limitations is your knowledge and experience, both of the sector and the role in which you work. For example, if you work in Human Resources, do you have sufficient knowledge of employment law? Reflect on your skills and knowledge: they may be good enough for your current role, but will they suffice in the future? Try to identify the role that best fits with your ambitions, and ask yourself what skills you will need to fit that role. Published job descriptions and job advertisements provide a good guide to current industry standards and what employers are looking for. Set about gaining those skills through additional training, or by realigning your role with your current employer.

SWOT analysis for a Human Resources executive

STRENGTHS
- O Experience in **training**
- O **Presentation** skills
- O Good **communicator**
- O Good **knowledge** of employment law

WEAKNESSES
- O Poor **understanding** of recruitment systems
- O No **experience** of disciplinary meetings
- O Don't like **conflict**

OPPORTUNITIES
- O Set up my own **training business**
- O **Broaden** my role to include recruitment

THREATS
- O Company may **outsource** training
- O Company may want all-round **HR skills** in the future

Carrying out a SWOT analysis

A simple way to assess yourself is to carry out a SWOT analysis. List your strengths and weaknesses, and the opportunities open and threats to you in your current role, as in the example above. This SWOT analysis provides a picture of the development you need to excel in your present situation, and the skills, knowledge, and experience you will need to acquire to succeed in your next professional role.

Developing your brand

We have looked at the importance of how other people see you and of understanding yourself, your strengths and limitations, and your ambitions. Developing your brand is about how you bring these factors together, use them to differentiate yourself from other people, and develop your career.

Giving the right impression

A company brand is a unique and consistent set of values that underpins its product or service. Just as a company builds its brand, you need to know what you stand for and how you want to project yourself to others. You need to make sure the messages you give out are consistent with your personal brand.

This does not mean you should try to be something you aren't. Pretending may work for a short time but it will be impossible to keep up over a long period. Your "brand" has to be something that you are completely comfortable with. It should reflect your values and be uniquely yours.

> Paying attention to **your appearance**, whatever your style, **being polite, and fulfilling your promises** are all "musts"

Creating the right look

There are some aspects of the way you look, sound, and behave that are essential to your brand, wherever you are working. Paying attention to your appearance, whatever your style, being polite, and fulfilling your promises, for

Tip

FOLLOW YOUR CUSTOMERS' LEAD
Match your **personal style** to that of your customers – it will help you **create rapport** with them.

example, are all "musts". Your brand needs to take into account your "target audience", such as the organization you work for and the customers you work with. If you work for an old-fashioned firm of lawyers, for example, wearing the latest fashion in shorts and flashy jewellery probably won't inspire your clients with confidence, but it may do if you work for a high-fashion retailer.

Being personable

While appearance is important, how you behave becomes far more important as time progresses. If you look the part but fail to do what you have been asked or are bad-tempered and difficult, then no amount of image makeovers will help you succeed. The key to defining your brand is to pay attention to every element of the image you project, and make sure your actions are consistent and acceptable to the majority of people.

What defines your brand?

LOOKING THE PART

- O The **clothes, shoes, and jewellery** you wear – style and colours
- O The way you **style your hair** – always well groomed
- O The way you **move – with a purpose**
- O The appearance of your **hands and nails** – clean at all times; if you wear nail polish, it should be appropriate to your situation

ACTING THE PART

- O **Shaking hands** firmly, but not squeezing too hard
- O Saying **thank you**
- O Returning **phone calls or emails** within a reasonable time
- O **Respecting** other people's views
- O Giving other people the **credit due** to them
- O Doing what you have **promised** to do
- O **Standing your ground** when necessary

SOUNDING THE PART

- O The **tone of your voice** – lower-pitched voices carry more weight
- O The **pace of your speech** – slow enough to sound purposeful but not hesitant
- O The **words you choose** – short, active, and positive, or longer and more descriptive?
- O The **expression in your voice** – approachable and friendly

Planning the future

There is a saying that "all plans are useless, but planning is vital". Plans are useless as they become out of date very quickly. But without the process of planning, you won't prepare for the future. You do need to plan, but don't stick to your plans so rigidly that you miss opportunities.

Knowing where you're going

Life is unpredictable, so why plan? First, all of the things you want to achieve in your life require effort and preparation. So, you need to ensure you acquire the qualifications and experience that will allow you to progress in your chosen career, and to do that, you need a plan. Having a plan gives you a framework against which to measure your progress.

Setting objectives

Have you achieved what you set out to do? If not, why not? What can you learn from your successes and failures? A plan also provides a reference against which you can judge new opportunities. How much will this opportunity contribute to you achieving your goals? If it doesn't, why do you want to do it? Is it a distraction or have your goals and plan changed?

In focus

WHAT'S ON YOUR CV?

One good way to plan the future is to create a version of your CV three, five, and ten years in the future. What qualifications would appear? What job titles would you have? Which companies would you have worked for? What experience would you have gained in each of the roles you have undertaken? If you don't know what to put on the CV, why not look in the papers or on the internet for job advertisements. They will tell you what people are looking for when filling these roles today. Although this won't change dramatically, certain aspects, such as qualifications, computer literacy, and international experience, will be more in demand. So by looking at the job requirements today and thinking about the future, you should be able to construct an outline future CV to work towards.

HAVING AN EFFECTIVE FUTURE PLAN

Dos	Don'ts
O Defining key measurable goals that logically lead to achieving your vision	O Relying on chance rather than your own efforts
O Setting goals that are believable and achievable	O Choosing goals with unattainable qualifiers (e.g. needing to be born in a certain country)
O Always using your plan when making big real-life decisions	O Reviewing and revising your plan infrequently

The things you want **to achieve** in your life require **effort and preparation**

Creating a plan

A good plan for your future needs to include four key elements:

- A vision statement that describes where you want to be
- A set of objectives that, if achieved, will lead you to the vision
- A "success map" showing how these objectives link together
- An indicator describing what success will look like at each stage.

Think first about your vision of the future: is it all about a single goal, such as becoming president of a multi-national company, or is it about a lifestyle, such as being a wealthy and respected partner in a law firm? Use some of the exercises described over the previous pages to help you to think about your vision. Next, write your vision down in a vision statement. This should not be longer than a paragraph, but needs to contain all the attributes that are important to you. Spend time on this statement; it is the important first step in planning your future.

> Write your vision down in a **vision statement**. This should not be longer than a paragraph, but needs to contain all **the attributes** that are **important** to you

Developing a vision

Once you have a clear idea of your overall vision for the future, break it down into its main constituent parts. Do this by creating a set of top-level objectives you will need to achieve to reach your vision.

ASK YOURSELF...
Am I on track to reach my goal?   **YES   NO**

Create an indicator of success for each of the objectives in your success map by asking yourself:

1 **Do I understand** why this objective is important? .... ☐ ☐

2 Do I know how it links into my **success map**? .... ☐ ☐

3 Can I identify **what is to be achieved** and by when? .... ☐ ☐

4 Can I **measure** this? .... ☐ ☐

5 Do I know how often I should **reflect on progress**? .... ☐ ☐

6 **Do I know what I should do** if the objective is not being met? .... ☐ ☐

20%

of people **write** New Year **goals**; they are **10 times** more likely to achieve them than those who do not

3%

of a group of Harvard MBA graduates **wrote down** their **goals**; **10 years** later they earned **10 times** more than those who did not

Creating a success map for your future

A success map is a useful tool for thinking through the key actions you need to take to achieve your goals and for representing these in a single picture.

- To create your success map start from the top – your ultimate goal. Write this at the top of your map.
- Think about how you will achieve this goal. For example, imagine your vision is to become sales director for a major pharmaceutical company. To achieve this goal, you will need to have been a regional sales manager for three to five years, to have handled some major clients within your portfolio, and to have gained a professional sales qualification. These objectives become the second-level goals on your success map.
- Next, ask yourself how to achieve these objectives, and fill in the next level of your map.
- At all stages, use arrows to connect later objectives that are dependent on you having first achieved the earlier objectives.
- To check that your success map is complete and follows a logical progression, work up from the bottom. For each objective, ask "Why am I doing this?" – the answer should be to obtain the objective above.

To become sales **director**, you will need to have been a **regional sales manager** for **three to five years** and **gained** a sales qualification

Success map for an aspiring sales director

Raise my profile within the company

Spend a secondment in brand marketing

Attend the Sales Management programme

Spead five years as a sales executive

Develop an excellent sales record

Pass the Institute's exams

55%
of US workers have planned a **five-year career** strategy

Spend **three to five years** as regional **sales manager**

Handle **large accounts** and have **major clients** within my portfolio

Achieve promotion to the level of **national sales director**

Obtain the relevant **professional sales qualification**

40%
of UK workers have planned a **five-year career** strategy with **clear goals**

Improving
your skills

Think of your portfolio of skills as your toolkit. Just like a good set of tools, once you have acquired your skills, they will always stay with you – as long as you maintain them. From time to time you will need to add new tools to your kit as the requirements of your job change or evolve, and as new ways of doing things emerge.

Managing your time

While you can raise additional finance for your business, employ more people, and buy more machinery, there will only ever be 24 hours in a day. Time is one of the few commodities you cannot buy, but there are many techniques to help you use your time more effectively.

How to set up a time log

> Planning **encourages you to think** not just about the day ahead, but also the **more distant future**

At the end of the week, analyze how you have spent your time and draw a pie chart to show where your time goes.

Tracking your time

Before you can start actively managing your time, you need to find out how you spend it. Rather than just guessing, measure and record your expenditure of time over a period of at least a week in a time log. When you have completed the analysis, consider if the way you spend time reflects your key objectives. For example, you may find that you spend five per cent of your time visiting customers. Is this activity one that delivers key results (because it generates sales)? If it is, you need to consider whether you would be more effective by spending more time on this activity.

As you work, record in the right -hand column the letter of the activity you have completed in the last 15 minutes.

Categorize your tasks, e.g. answering emails, writing reports, planning, thinking, visiting clients, travelling.

30%
of workers do not **make or use** a **"to do" list**

Assign a code or letter to each of these categories (e.g. emails = E, thinking = T).

Keep a sheet of paper on your desk, divided into two columns.

Split your day into 15-minute segments; enter these periods in the first column.

Making time
Planning encourages you to think not just about the day ahead, but also the more distant future. It's all too easy to put off big but necessary strategic projects, such as arranging training for your staff or creating a database of contacts, because you are immersed in day-to-day activities. Think about the longer-term projects you would like to implement in the next quarter. Break these tasks into manageable chunks, and estimate how much time it will take you to complete each chunk.

Planning your day

Write an action plan setting out your activities for the day ahead. The best time to do this is at the beginning of the day, when you feel fresh. Build time into your plan for day-to-day duties and the work you need to do towards your longer-term projects. Failing to stick to an over-optimistic plan can be demotivating, so be realistic in your timings, allowing for interruptions and some breaks.

Calculating priority

When writing your plan, prioritize your tasks objectively – it often helps to categorize tasks according to importance and urgency. Give priority to those that are both urgent and important (for example, producing up-to-date figures for the next day's sales meeting). Tasks that are important but not urgent (such as completing segments of your large projects) take second priority. Tasks that are not important but urgent (such as dealing with someone else's request for information) take third priority, and those that are neither important nor urgent should be delegated or not done at all.

> **Categorize tasks** according to **importance and urgency**. Give **priority** to those that are both urgent and important. Tasks that are important but not urgent take **second priority**

Tip

BE DISCIPLINED
Try to **deal with paperwork** only once. Mark a red dot on a document each time you pick it up; attempt to minimize the number of red dots on your paperwork – **the discipline will slowly work** its way into all your processes.

How to prioritize your tasks

40%

of **productivity** is estimated to be lost due to workers visiting **non-work related websites** during office hours

Structuring your day

To make the most of every work day, get to know the times of day when you are most effective and creative. If you are a "morning" person, plan to tackle your creative tasks – such as writing proposals or reports – and your challenging tasks, such as talking to a difficult client, in the morning. Take on routine tasks in the afternoon. If you are an "afternoon" person, do your routine tasks first, but make sure that you don't get hooked into doing them all day.

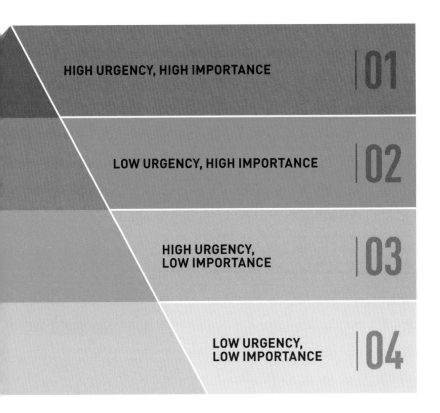

HIGH URGENCY, HIGH IMPORTANCE 01

LOW URGENCY, HIGH IMPORTANCE 02

HIGH URGENCY, LOW IMPORTANCE 03

LOW URGENCY, LOW IMPORTANCE 04

Working effectively

To help you work quickly and effectively, always keep your desk tidy and ensure frequently used items are readily available to hand. The same goes for information you use regularly. Set up favourites for websites; keep a list of who knows what, and of key phone numbers; and use an old-fashioned card index for storing nuggets of information you refer to often.

Build thinking time into your schedule: travel is often considered to be a time-waster, but it can also provide just the change of pace and scenery you need to do some valuable creative thinking.

Set aside **15 minutes** every so often to **collect messages and return calls**. Let people know you will be unavailable between certain times

Focusing your actions

TELEPHONE CALLS

O **Prepare everything** you want to say before you call.

O **Talking on the telephone** helps to build relationships, but sometimes emailing instead avoids distraction.

O **If someone calls** you and you're short on time, tell them you will call them back at a specific time. Be sure always to follow up on your promise.

90% of **office workers** have a **smartphone** and **33% of them** use it to check their **emails** more than **20 times every day**, during **working hours and at home**

Dealing with interruptions

Make sure the working day is under your control by eliminating interruptions at key times. If you are working on a report that requires concentration, divert your phone or put it on voicemail; set aside 15 minutes every so often to collect messages and return calls. Let people know you will be unavailable between certain times. If someone drops in to talk to you at an unexpected time, tell them you are working to a deadline and avoid making eye contact – they will get the message.

EMAILS

- O **Streamline** your use of email by checking for new messages and responding to them only at certain times of the day.

- O **Use colour** to highlight important or urgent emails.

- O **Target emails:** avoid copying in people you don't need to, and ask others to do the same.

- O **Clear out** your email inbox regularly.

WORKING QUICKLY

- O **Make your decision** and don't keep thinking about it afterwards.

- O **Balance time** with quality control; a report may be excellent, but if it's too late it may be of no use.

- O **Concentrate** on what you're doing at a particular time, and don't let your thoughts flit from one thing to another.

Participating in meetings

It's easy to forget the importance of meetings. This is where decisions are made that could affect your work and your future, where relationships are built, and where you have an opportunity to make an impression on others, make your views heard, and find out what others think.

Researching well

Preparation is essential to ensure you make the most of your opportunity. Read any material in advance and note down issues you need to clarify and points you want to make. For important and complex discussions, you may want to sound out other people's opinions to help you form your own view and get an idea of who will support your thinking.

Making your mark

When you arrive at a meeting try to sit near people who are likely to support your views, and ideally in the middle rather than at the end of the group. During the meeting, it is very important to find opportunities to speak. If you are nervous about making your own points, get used to hearing your voice by making short remarks in support of others. A clear, firm: "I agree with that point" will get you noticed. Also, ask questions for clarification, which will make you sound interested. Try drafting some points to make in advance, and introduce them early in the discussion, but make sure that you do so in the context of the discussion. Be careful, too, that you don't speak too much: it's better to be known as someone who makes good points than who speaks all the time.

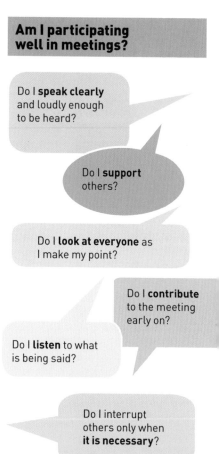

Am I participating well in meetings?

Do I **speak clearly** and loudly enough to be heard?

Do I **support** others?

Do I **look at everyone** as I make my point?

Do I **contribute** to the meeting early on?

Do I **listen** to what is being said?

Do I interrupt others only when **it is necessary**?

Recording meetings

Minutes should be produced for all meetings, even if they are just simple notes of who agreed to do what. For regular meetings, such as staff meetings or committee meetings, it can be useful if they take a formal style, because this helps to reinforce the importance of the meeting.

Taking minutes

If you are the minute-taker, clarify what form the minutes should take with the chairperson. For some meetings it is important to know who said what. In that case you may need to place name plates in front of each of the attendees. For most meetings, however, the key point is to record actions you decide on, who is taking them, and when they must be completed. If the chairperson does not summarize what has been agreed at the end of each agenda item, ask them for further clarification. Always aim to produce the minutes as soon as possible after the meeting, when the discussion is fresh in your mind. Try to keep the minutes as succinct as possible, without detracting from making a full and accurate record of everything that had been agreed.

Tip

MAKE YOURSELF HEARD

Have the **first words** of what you want to say in your mind; **wait** for a pause, then **say those words clearly**. Pause, then carry on with the rest.

CHECKLIST...

Generating formal minutes of a meeting

		YES	NO
1	Have you stated the **"title" of the meeting,** where it took place, and when?	☐	☐
2	Have you **listed the people** who were present at the meeting, and those who apologized for their absence?	☐	☐
3	Have you **agreed and noted** that the minutes of the last meeting were an accurate record of what happened?	☐	☐
4	Have you **given a description** of any additional discussion points that arose from the minutes of the last meeting?	☐	☐
5	Have you **detailed each agenda point,** describing what was discussed and what decisions were made?	☐	☐
6	Have you **highlighted** the action points, and stated who will be completing each task and by when?	☐	☐

Chairing a meeting

Chairing a meeting is an excellent way to gain visibility. You don't need to have expertise in the subject of the meeting, but you do have to develop a range of procedural skills. These range from the technical – how to produce an agenda – to the diplomatic, such as how to keep the discussion moving and stop participants from speaking for too long.

How to run the meeting

Ensure there is someone to take the minutes and let them know the format you want the minutes to follow.

At the end of the meeting, remind everyone what has to be achieved and summarize what has been agreed, to help the minute-taker.

Calling a meeting

People often complain about how many meetings they have to attend. At a time when few of us have time to spare, going to a meeting that results in no action is just a waste of time. So before you call a meeting, ask yourself: is this meeting necessary or can it be done by another means, such as by email or a conference call perhaps?

Inviting the right people

If you do decide that a meeting is necessary, next consider who should attend. This will obviously depend on the purpose of the meeting. If you are briefing employees about changes that are to be made to your department's structure, for example, then it's essential that everyone attends. If you want views on how the structure should change, on the other hand, you might want to invite just a few key people. Once you have decided who should attend, send out notices of the date and place in plenty of time. Give an indication of how long the meeting will take, to help your invitees plan their time.

Setting the agenda

An agenda is essential to ensure that your meeting has a focus and to enable participants to prepare beforehand. How you structure it will have a major impact on the success of the meeting. The best plan is to word the agenda so that the type of treatment necessary for each item is clear.

> A **successful chairperson** is able to make **everyone feel** that their **opinions have been valued**

Let everyone speak, but move the conversation on to the next person when they have had their say.

If someone is dominating the discussion, politely say "Thank you. That was useful and I think we've understood your point. I see Joe has something to add."

Keep to time, but allow sufficient airing of the issues.

Try to bring quieter people into the conversation. If you think someone may have something to contribute, ask directly if he or she would like to add anything.

Creating items

An item labelled "To discuss" on an agenda, means an open debate of the issues. The term "To note", means there will not be any real general discussion unless there is a point someone is desperate to raise. The timings you allot to each item and where you place items on the agenda will give participants an idea of the importance of that subject. For regular meetings, it is usually a good idea to ask participants in advance if there is anything they want to add to the agenda, or whether there is anything they want to raise under "any other business".

Running the meeting

The role of the chairperson is to ensure the meeting achieves its aims. There are a number of key techniques for doing this. One of the main characteristics of a successful chairperson is being able to make everyone feel they have been able to air their views, that their opinions have been valued, and that they have achieved something.

Negotiating

Negotiating is all about bargaining to reach a mutually agreeable outcome. It is a skill that will give you an enduring advantage, not just at work, but in almost every aspect of your life. The keys to success in any negotiation are having clear objectives and being thoroughly prepared.

Knowing your ideal

A negotiation involves two (or more) parties, who have different needs, agreeing to compromise in order for something to happen. Preparation is vital: start by formulating a clear understanding of what you want to achieve, what you are prepared to concede, and how you will go about the process. Think about what you want the outcome of the negotiation to be, discussing and agreeing it with others where necessary.

| 01 **TIME IT RIGHT**

Start negotiating only when you are ready to do a deal. Don't begin the process on a fact-finding trip, for example.

Strategies for successful negotiation

55% of workers surveyed said they **taught** themselves **how to negotiate**; 9% learned from **a mentor**

02 TEST OUT YOUR TECHNIQUE

Practise your negotiating technique in situations where the outcome is not too significant.

04 OFFER TRADES

Propose trades with the other party: "If you could see your way to do this, we might be able to pay cash in advance."

03 LOOK FROM THE OTHER SIDE

Make a list of what you think the other side see as their must-haves, ideals, and give-aways.

05 SUMMARIZE AS YOU GO ALONG

At each stage, restate what has been discussed: "So, we have agreed that..."

06 DON'T MOVE TOO SOON

Make sure that everything is on the table before you decide to make an offer.

08 DON'T BE FOOLED

If something looks too good to be true, it probably is – don't be taken in by slick sales patter.

07 MAKE YOUR OFFER

When you have reached a position, make a clear offer and wait for a clear response.

Structuring your approach

Break down your thoughts into three areas:

- The must-haves: these are the essential aspects of the deal – if they are not available, you will walk away.
- The ideal: this describes your perfect deal and defines all the elements that contribute to it.
- The give-aways: these are the aspects of the deal that you would be prepared to trade for your "must-have" or ideal components.

"must-haves"

"ideals"

"give-aways"

Being prepared

Before you start any negotiation, it is crucial that you understand what else is on offer. Before you attempt to buy a car, for example, you need to have visited other showrooms to see what is available and for how much, and to have looked at the road-test report, price guides, and reviews. You also need to understand what you are buying. When you buy a mobile phone, the price may seem very reasonable, but you may be locked into a 12- or 18-month contract. So, unpack the product or service and understand all the aspects.

86%

of employees in one survey said that they **wished to learn** how to **negotiate a better salary**

NEGOTIATING YOURSELF A BETTER SALARY

The best time to negotiate your salary is before you accept a job. Your prospective employer has invested money in recruitment advertising or consultants, and taken time selecting you. You are in a strong position until you accept, especially if you have received other job offers too. In these situations push for what you really think you're worth. Remember that every subsequent pay rise will be based on that initial agreement, so getting it right will influence your salary for many years to come.

Gaining power

Such analysis helps in two ways. First, it helps you to identify your "must-haves", "ideals", and "give-aways". Second, it gives you negotiating power. If you can drop information about competitors into the negotiation, it forces the other party to respond in some way, giving you an advantage.

"must-haves"

"ideals"

"give-aways"

Analysis helps in two ways. First, it helps you to **identify** your "must-haves", "ideals", and "give-aways". Second, it gives you **negotiating power**

Tip

BE CLEAR

Make sure that you **clarify** all statements made by the other party. Ambiguity is the enemy of **good negotiation**.

Doing the deal

Nearly every major negotiation requires a meeting. When you enter a negotiation meeting, you will have your objectives, but be prepared to modify your stance in the ebb and flow of the bargaining. As the discussion progresses, the other party will give you clues that indicate their position. For example, if their tone becomes more reflective, they may be about to concede a point, so ease off to give them the time and space to make the step.

Understanding body language

Look out for body language that reveals what the other person is thinking. If the other person leans away from you, for example, it may indicate disinterest, or a demonstration of superiority: try to engage your counterpart more, without being confrontational. If more than one negotiator is present, watch the person who is not speaking. Directing some of your questions to them may open up other avenues.

Giving a reason

Most good negotiators know they have to explain why they want something, and that they have to give the other person a reason to agree. However, research has shown that the logic behind the reason itself does not necessarily have to be complex or detailed. Basic as it may seem, if you can back up your argument with even a simple reason, you are much more likely to convince your counterpart to agree to your proposal.

CASE STUDY

RENEGOTIATING TERMS

The managing director of a window manufacturer was introduced to a potential new customer, a small company wanting to buy window frames. A deal was negotiated based on payment with order, so there was no credit risk. The sales manager and MD had a good feeling about the new customer. They received the order for the end of the week and put it into manufacture early to make sure it was ready for a Friday collection. But on Thursday night, the sales manager received a call from the customer saying they had hit a problem with their finance company, which had delayed the release of the money. Could they put back the order a week?

The windows had already been made, and could not be sold elsewhere. There was little to be lost and much to be gained by allowing the customer to have credit on this order. If they were dishonest, it would be better to find out sooner rather than later, but if things were as they said, the new relationship would be strengthened. The customers were as good as their word and paid a week later. The trust created by this one act resulted in a flow of future orders.

NEGOTIATING SUCCESSFULLY

Dos	Don'ts
O Stating your requirements clearly so the other party understands your position	O Neglecting your preparation – if you don't plan you won't succeed
O Being patient and accepting that negotiations take time	O Giving way on a point you know you can't concede
O Demonstrating empathy with the other party	O Becoming confrontational, or showing aggression
O Ending positively, even if you don't get exactly what you want	O Continuing to negotiate after the deal is agreed

Reaching agreement

Once you have reached a position, offer it to the other side unambiguously and clearly. Wait in silence until they respond. They may ask for clarification or negotiate on a small issue, but if they raise a whole new issue, something is amiss: ask for an adjournment and reconsider the deal from scratch. When the deal is agreed, do not go back on it except under exceptional circumstances. People will not trust you again if you just change your mind, without giving some very good reasons.

When **the deal is agreed**, don't **go back** on it

Dealing with difficult people

A difficult person could be someone who is genuinely obstructive or just an individual who sees the world differently from you. In either case, to manage difficult behaviour, you first need to gain an understanding of the person, and then employ a set of tactics to manage the situation.

Planning for resolution

You can't change a difficult person by being difficult yourself. You have to set a target for the situation or relationship you wish to achieve, and then create a strategy to reach that goal. The approach you take will depend on the situation, the person, and the type of behaviour. One option is to call a private meeting with the difficult individual

Tip

ACT EARLY
Tackle difficult behaviour as soon as it **becomes evident** – the longer you leave it, the harder it becomes to cope with, and it may affect other members of the team.

Discussing the situation

Select a location to meet in a place where you won't be disturbed or noticed by colleagues. Prepare what you want to say and how you will say it. Tell the person how you see the main issues and problem, logically and without emotion. Ask how the individual sees it – don't interrupt, even if you disagree. Ask for solutions and, finally, add some ways in which you think the problems might be resolved.

Facing up to conflict

Truly difficult people are difficult with everyone. Few will fail to notice their behaviour, so it is important to face any conflict rather that allowing it to fester and affect the whole team. It is important to keep in mind that you need to act and not let the conflict affect you deeply. If the other person becomes threatening or abusive, walk away with dignity, saying you will consider the situation and get back to him or her.

CONDUCTING A MEETING

Dos	Don'ts
O Letting the person speak	O Interrupting
O Putting your case calmly	O Getting over-emotional
O Standing your ground	O Becoming argumentative
O Breathing slowly and deeply	O Taking it personally

Strategies for difficult behaviours

TYPE OF BEHAVIOUR	COPING STRATEGY
Negative Complains and disagrees with everything	O **Keep positive** – avoid being dragged down to their level O Point out **earlier instances** where your **suggestion has worked** O Put their **"trouble-spotting" talents** to good use on a project of their own
Unresponsive Uses silence as an offensive weapon	O **Allow silences**, rather than filling gaps in the conversation O Get them to talk by **asking open questions** to which they can't answer just "yes" or "no" O If you can't get them talking, call the meeting to a halt. **Explain** that nothing is being achieved and **propose another meeting** or course of action. Ask them to consider how the situation might be resolved
Overpowering Uses anger as an offensive weapon	O Let them **express** their anger O Try to **empathize** O When they have calmed down, **find the real cause** and possible solutions
Wants to "go it alone" Doesn't see themself as part of the team	O Tell them how they are seen by other **team members** O **Explain** what team membership requires O Point out how their **strengths can help** the team
Shows enthusiasm but few results Underachieves repeatedly	O Without dampening their **enthusiasm**, ask why something hasn't been completed O Help them **understand** how to get things done O Restrict their **workload**

Presenting

It is wholly possible to become successful and achieve high performance without being good at speaking in public. However, presentations give you an unrivalled opportunity to shine and, most of all, become visible within your organization. There are two aspects to learning how to present well: the psychological side, overcoming your fear; and the process side, learning the techniques to do it well.

Being prepared

Successful speakers make delivering a presentation look effortless. In fact, the opposite is true: the key to speaking well is all about exhaustive preparation and practice. You need to get the content right, plan how to deliver it, and then rehearse until you are entirely confident with your speech. Before you plan the content of the presentation in great detail, make sure that you know:

● Who your audience are, what they need from you, and how much background information they will need
● How much time you have for your talk, including question time
● What audio-visual equipment is available
● How the seating for delegates will be arranged in the room.

> The **key** to **speaking well** is exhaustive **preparation** and **practice**. You need to get the **content** right

Planning your presentation

| 01
SET OBJECTIVES

Decide what your **objectives** are – what do you want **the audience** to take away with them?

| 04
PLAN THE INTRODUCTION

Describe what you will be covering in the presentation, **setting the scene** and preparing your audience for what is to come.

| 07
PLAN TRANSITIONS

Plan how you will **"signpost"** the start of each section – this helps your listeners **concentrate and remember** what you have said.

| 02
SET THE STRUCTURE

Structure your talk in **three sections:** scene setting, the main content, and a summary.

| 03
MAKE NOTES

Jot down notes for each section, keeping **detail brief** and only focusing on the **key issues**.

| 05
MAP OUT THE MAIN CONTENT

Be selective about what you include. It is better to make three or four key points than try to rush through too much information.

| 06
WRITE THE SUMMARY

In the summary, briefly go over **the main points** that your talk has covered and **emphasize** any actions that need to be taken.

| 08
SUMMARIZE YOUR NOTES

Write out your presentation, using **bullet points** or short sentences, on **small cards** that are easy to handle.

| 09
USE COLOUR

Colour code your notes to help you **quickly identify** the transitions between different sections.

Practising your delivery

Research has shown that your voice – how you say something – is better remembered than the words you use, so practise how you deliver your speech. Begin by standing up, both feet firmly on the floor. Don't be too rigid and don't hunch, because you will smother your voice. Move your head gently from side to side to help you relax.

Speaking with conviction

When you speak, imagine your voice reaching the very back of the room like a wave rolling on to a beach. Voice control isn't just about projection: you need to add expression, depth, and resonance. Vary the pace of your speech to make it interesting. Cast your mind back to speakers you have heard who talk in a monotone – it's very difficult to concentrate on what they are saying without letting your mind wander. One of the best ways to practise putting expression and interest into your voice is to read children's stories aloud.

How you say something is **better remembered** than the **words** you use

Think about the visuals

Are your **slides clean, clutter free**, and **consistent** in their style and typeface?

Do you have too many slides? As a general rule, **aim** for no more than **one or two slides per minute**.

Tip

LEARN FROM THE GREATS
Take **every opportunity** to listen to the **speeches of the great orators**. Concentrate on their delivery. Notice how they **grab your attention**, how they use silence to give emphasis, and how they **vary the tone and pace** of their speech.

Voice control isn't just about **projection**: you need to **add expression**, **depth**, and **resonance**

Do **your slides** include too much data? Restrict the **numbers and words** on each slide to a few key facts.

Do your **visuals** – slides, photographs, or props – **add sufficient value** to your words?

Going with the flow

Giving a presentation is a two-way process. You may be the person at the front of the room doing most of the talking, but the audience will be giving non-verbal feedback all the time. Try to catch the eyes of people around the room throughout the presentation. Smile occasionally during your talk, but don't adopt a false, fixed grin.

Move around and use gestures if that feels natural for you. The more relaxed and natural you appear, the more rapport you will be able to create. Be careful not to move around too much, though, because it can make you seem nervous.

Coping with problems

If something does go wrong, such as your papers falling off the table or the bulb in the projector failing, take a deep breath.

Techniques to help calm your nerves

- Banish negative "what will happen if..." thoughts. If you have prepared well, you needn't worry.
- Visit the venue ahead of time and familiarize yourself with the room you will present in.
- Stand at the podium and imagine the room full of people. Say a few words to get used to how your voice sounds.
- Visualize yourself delivering your presentation confidently and the audience applauding.
- Use relaxation techniques to keep you calm as the time of your talk approaches. For example, think about each part of your body, from your feet upwards, and imagine you are tensing and then relaxing that part.
- Say to yourself: "I can do this!"
- Picture a relaxing scene that you can call up if nerves threaten to get the better of you – practise this beforehand.

Unless they are very unusual people, your audience will empathize with you, because its something nearly everyone dreads. If it's something you can remedy quickly, look at the audience, smile, and put the matter right. If it's a more difficult problem like fixing the projector bulb, look out for the organizers, and ask for their help. In the meantime, try to carry on with the talk as best you can. You will be remembered for coping well.

Dealing with interruptions

If you are interrupted, listen to the point being made and answer it briefly. Say you'll deal with it later or will speak to that person afterwards, then put the incident out of your mind.

> The more **relaxed** you appear, the more **rapport** you will create

- When it is time for you to start, walk confidently to the podium and smile at the audience.
- Take a moment to put your papers down purposefully.
- Focus on what you are saying: it drowns out negative thoughts.
- Keep your feet firmly on the floor.
- Speak slowly – it is easy to speak too fast when you are nervous.
- Keep breathing! Occasionally take a slow, deep breath.

- If you feel an attack of nerves, pick a friendly face in the audience and smile at them.
- Remember that no-one in the audience wants you to fail.

> **You** may be doing the talking, but the **audience** will be giving **non-verbal** feedback

Becoming
more effective

There is a basic set of skills that can help you become more effective at everything you do. Like the oil in a machine, skills such as listening, decision-making, and communicating can help you work more smoothly and be more successful.

03

Reading and remembering

We are bombarded with information all day. The key to success is to be able to identify what is important and then remember it. Recalling an important fact can make the difference between success or failure in the heat of a negotiation or an important meeting.

Reading rapidly

Reading a text book is not the same as reading for pleasure. There is a process for reading a text book. Start by reading the introduction, then read the last chapter. At this point you should know what the book is about and how it's structured; now, you can decide whether it's worth reading the rest. If you think you would benefit from reading the book, begin by looking at the headings and diagrams on each page; you will be surprised by how much you learn. Once you have done your initial review, leave a gap before you read the book as a whole – this greatly reinforces learning.

Scanning the details

The faster you read, the more you will remember. If you practise long enough, you will be able to scan a document and remember enough to hold a conversation about it. Start by reading whole sentences in one go. To do this, focus your eyes on the sentence rather than on each word. Move to looking at paragraphs. Soon you should be able to look at the page towards the top, in the middle, and finally at the bottom before you turn over.

300

words per minute
(wpm) is the average
reading rate. Skim
reading is **700 wpm** and
speed readers reach
over **4,000 wpm**

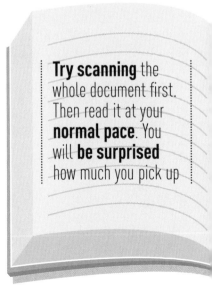

Try scanning the whole document first. Then read it at your **normal pace**. You will **be surprised** how much you pick up

Learning from documents

When you are learning, try scanning the whole document first. Then read it at your normal pace. Just scanning first will improve your understanding and memory. If you are late and unprepared for a meeting, try scanning some of your documents. You will be surprised how much you pick up. Even if it does not work, you will be able to find most of the information you need much more quickly.

Using mind maps

A mind map is an effective way to record information in a succinct format that you can easily remember. To create a mind map that summarizes the content of a book you have read, for example, start by writing the subject of the book in the centre of a sheet of paper. Then draw

In focus

REMEMBERING NAMES

Most people worry about remembering the names of the people they meet. If you have difficulty, try the following: when you are introduced, always repeat the person's name. While you are doing this, look into the individual's face and identify a feature that reminds you of their names. Does Sr. Marrón have brown hair, or is his hair so startlingly different that you will remember his name? If there isn't a feature that is memorable, try imagining the person acting their names – Julia Stokes the steam train, for example, or Paul Parsons giving the sermon.

branches radiating from the subject that sum up the major themes of the book. Next, fill in smaller branches containing the sub-themes, and finally add detail to these sub-themes in the outer "twigs" of your mind map.

Remembering the ideas

Use pictures and colour liberally, as they make your mind map more memorable and will increase your recall of the information. If you want to be sure that you will remember the content of your map, review it the day after you have drawn it, one week later, one month later, and finally one year later.

Being creative

Many problems have simple solutions, but those are the problems that everyone can solve. Being creative enables you to solve, or contribute to solving, difficult problems. This will get you noticed. Some people appear naturally creative, but creative problem-solving is a skill that you can learn and hone through practice.

Finding creative solutions

Creativity comes from abandoning linear thought and making leaps of the imagination. All your brain needs is the stimulus to make these leaps. Brainstorming is one technique for helping do this. Getting a group of people together to throw out possible solutions without the constraint of evaluating the suggestions creates energy and sparks new ideas. Another technique is asking people to consider

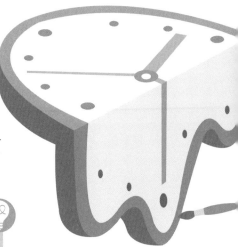

> **Tip**
>
> **STIMULATE CREATIVITY**
> Very few **good ideas** have been created by sitting alone at a desk. **Change your scene**, have a coffee and **relax**, or **interact with others**.

the problem from a different perspective, such as: "How will our customers see this?" or "What if we turn the question on its head?"

Practise being creative in your private life, and it will develop your ability to be creative at work. Stimulate your brain by taking a different route to work, completing crossword puzzles, learning a new language, taking an activity holiday, or finding a new experience.

Practise being **creative** in your private life, and it will **develop** your **ability** to be **creative at work**

Asking the right questions

When you are faced with a problem, it is often the boundaries or rules that constrain your thinking. "We can't do this because..." is a phrase that stifles creativity. Instead, asking the question: "What if this constraint wasn't there?" will allow you to consider all the new options and benefits open to you, and can create a new world in your mind. You will often find the opportunities open to you when you remove a constraint are so great that it is worth the time and effort it takes to remove it. Did James Dyson ask the question "What if we don't have a bag?" when he invented his revolutionary bagless vacuum cleaner?

Using benchmarking

Not every problem has to be solved again from scratch. Most problems have been solved before so all you have to do is find the solution. Benchmarking is a very useful tool for doing this.

Benchmarking is about comparing processes. It is about weighing up the way your organization does something against the way in which another organization performs the same function. Start by making sure that you understand your own processes. Who does what, when, how, and why? Just doing this will create ideas for improvement, but it also forms the basis for benchmarking: comparing your processes with those of your chosen benchmark subject.

Who should you benchmark yourself against? Ideally, find an organization that is really good at the process you are trying to improve – for example, if you want to improve your despatch function, you might benchmark yourself against a company that is efficient at dealing with complex orders.

Being confident

Confidence is precious. It enables you to do what you want to do without constant fear of failure, or even despite fear on some occasions, and to maintain your sense of self-worth and not be dependent on what other people think. If you're confident, you can take centre stage when you want – you don't always have to linger in the background.

Thinking positive

The first step in building your confidence is to pay attention to what you're thinking. Concentrate on your positive thoughts. It's very easy to focus on the negative. You probably find that when you have been given feedback, at your appraisal perhaps, you concentrate solely on the one negative comment even though there were five positive comments.

Creating good thoughts

To help overcome this, build a bank of achievements and positive comments that you can contemplate and reflect on whenever you feel uncertain about yourself and your abilities. Take some time to yourself and sit down with a pen and paper, and answer the following simple questions:

- What have I achieved in the last year and in the last five years?
- What am I most proud of? What did it feel like when I did it?
- What am I good at? Create a list of your talents and skills.
- What compliments have I received from others?

Concentrate solely on the positives of each situation, don't let negative "but" thoughts creep in. Commit the answers to your "achievement bank" and draw on them in moments of doubt.

Pay attention to what you're thinking. **Concentrate** on your **positive thoughts**

What have I **achieved** in the **last year** and in the **last five years**?

Focusing on others can create an **increase in confidence** of up to

67%

What am **I good at**?

What **compliments** have I **received from others**?

What am I **most proud of**? What did it **feel like** when I did it?

Case study

DRAWING ON EXPERIENCE

A young executive was given the authority by his boss, the group managing director, to negotiate the purchase of a company. This in itself was a daunting task, but, arriving at the meeting with a partner from the company's lawyers as his only colleague, he was ushered into a room to find 11 people sitting opposite. The owners of the company he was buying were there, as were their accountants, tax advisors, and lawyers, and three merchant bankers. For an instant, he was totally overwhelmed. Then he remembered an industrial relations negotiating course he had attended a few years before. He recalled how he had handled that situation successfully, his confidence immediately returned, and he successfully negotiated the deal.

Managing thoughts

Most of us have a voice in our heads telling us to be careful and stopping us from doing things that would cause harm to ourselves. The same voice can also prevent us from doing new things and progressing: "If you do this, you'll make a fool of yourself. Let someone else do it." When you hear that voice, ask yourself: "What's the worst that can happen if I do this?", "How likely is that to happen?", and "What's the best that can happen?" In most cases you will find the good outweighs the bad, and you should go ahead. If not, at least you will have evaluated the risk logically and assessed whether it is one you are prepared to take.

Looking confident

It is also important to build confidence on the outside – how you appear to others. Even if you don't feel it, "acting" confident can have an effect on both you and those around you. If you have a confident demeanour you are likely to be treated like a confident person by others. This will reinforce your self-belief and help you to feel more confident in yourself.

All of us get into bad habits, whether it's slumping in our seat, forgetting to acknowledge people when we meet them, or not taking enough care over our appearance. Take a moment to think about the image you portray – is it one of a confident and professional person?

CHECKLIST...
Appearing confident

		YES	NO
1	Do I maintain **good posture?** (An upright posture, keeping your shoulders down and your neck relaxed, makes you look and sound confident.)	☐	☐
2	Do I **control my breathing** when I'm nervous? (Fast, shallow breaths make you light-headed and raise the pitch of your voice, betraying your lack of confidence.)	☐	☐
3	Do I avoid closed **body language,** such as crossing my arms, and instead use open gestures and occupy the space around me as if I own it?	☐	☐
4	Do I **sit comfortably** rather than rigidly, avoiding jerky movements and fighting the urge to fidget?	☐	☐
5	Do I always **dress neatly and appropriately** and feel comfortable in what I wear?	☐	☐

"What's the
best
that can
happen?"

If you have a **confident demeanour** you are likely to be treated like a **confident person** by others

7 **years** may be added to the **lifespan** of **people** with positive thoughts

Making decisions

The place that you have reached in your career or your personal life is the result of the decisions you have made. Every decision closes off some opportunities and opens others. Life is full of difficult choices and that is why making good decisions is essential.

Defining the process

Making big decisions isn't simply about mulling over a few options. Big decisions require thought, information gathering, and the creation and evaluation of alternatives before the decision is finally taken. Timing is critical: you may sometimes be able to delay a major decision – although think carefully through the consequences if you do – but for many you will have to seize the moment.

Deciding process

When faced with a major decision, use the process described here to give structure to your decision-making. This will work for large personal decisions that you take yourself, but is even more important if you are working with others in making the decision.

> **Tip**
>
> **GO WITH THE FLOW**
> If your **company culture** is for decisions to be made by **consensus**, do that. If you **act alone,** you will not be supported and are likely to fail, regardless of whether the decision you made was correct or not.

Use **the process** described here to give **structure** to your **decision-making**

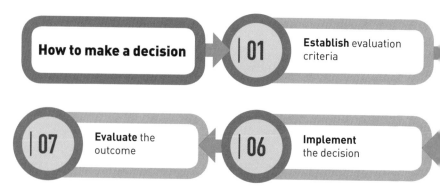

How to make a decision

| 01 Establish evaluation criteria

| 07 Evaluate the outcome

| 06 Implement the decision

Making group decisions

Group decision-making can be very powerful, as it creates ownership of the decision. Make sure that all involved understand the process you will use, and are aware of the input that is required at each stage. The decision will even be supported by those who disagree with the outcome, as long as the process by which you have made the decision is seen to be transparent and fair. However, you will have to abide by the outcome of the process. If you fail to do so, the decision may be seen as arbitrary and the team will be reluctant to be involved again.

38%

of employees claimed they valued their **own judgement** of an **analysis** when making **business decisions**

Establishing criteria

There are two reasons to establish early on the criteria by which you will evaluate your decision. First, these criteria will determine what information you need to collect to make the decision. Second, they help make the decision process transparent. Everyone involved knows what the list of alternatives will be judged against.

Prioritizing elements

In joint decisions, create and agree the evaluation criteria in a group. Your organization will have its own criteria, so make sure these are included on the list. If the result is a very long list, then persuade the group to agree and prioritize the most important criteria for making the decision.

In business, the evaluation criteria are often hard numbers – to do something for the least cost, for example, or to make the most profit. In your personal life, the criteria are usually more subjective – the relative size of the property you are buying, or the desirability of its location. Often you need both types, which is why you need to use judgement.

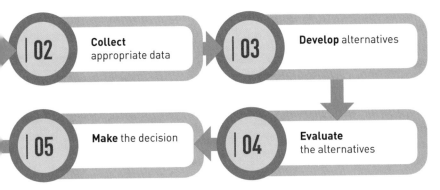

| 02 Collect appropriate data → 03 Develop alternatives ↓ 05 Make the decision ← 04 Evaluate the alternatives

Finding alternatives

Decisions are usually choices between alternatives; so successful decision-making depends on identifying the best possible set of alternatives to evaluate. Search widely, but remember you can't evaluate everything. You may need to be creative and on occasions "to think the unthinkable", but don't forget the obvious.

One alternative you should consider is doing nothing. This is not always easy, but may be a real alternative. At the very least it gives you a benchmark against which to compare the other possibilities. In some circumstances you may find it is possible to do two of the alternatives at the same time. This will require greater levels of evaluation than discussed here, but asking the question can sometimes overcome major dilemmas.

43%

of **employees** in one survey **valued analysis** more than judgement in decision-making

Decision chart for choosing between two houses

House purchase decision

BUY HOUSE A:
BORROW £300,000

Likely interest rate	Annual mortgage cost	Chance of interest rate	Proportion of cost
10%	£30,000	20%	£6,000
6%	£18,000	50%	£9,000
4%	£12,000	30%	£3,600
House A total expected annual mortgage cost			**£18,600**

Using decision charts

Creating a decision diagram or chart can help you weigh up alternatives. For example, imagine you are considering buying a house and have found two options, one of which is more expensive than the other. To buy house A, you will need to borrow £300,000; to buy house B, £500,000. You are concerned about how much each of the houses will cost you to buy over the lifetime of your mortgage. To compare the two options, first consider what the interest rates are likely to be in the future. For example, you may evaluate three possibilities: interest rates rising to 10 per cent, staying at the current rate of 6 per cent, and falling to 4 per cent. Next estimate the percentage chance of each change happening. For both houses there is a 50 per cent chance of the rate remaining at 6 per cent.

Now create your decision chart. To calculate the expected cost, multiply the annual mortgage cost by the percentage chance for each interest rate and then total the costs. The expected annual mortgage cost for house A is £18,600 and £31,000 for house B.

Use this information to evaluate your alternatives, but remember that this is the average expected cost. Averages rarely happen, so you also need to assess risk, by asking yourself: "Can I afford the house if the interest rates are at 10 per cent for a long period?"

BUY HOUSE B: BORROW £500,000

Likely interest rate	Annual mortgage cost	Chance of interest rate	Proportion of cost
10%	£50,000	20%	£10,000
6%	£30,000	50%	£15,000
4%	£20,000	30%	£6,000
House B total expected annual mortgage cost			**£31,000**

Making the decision

By the time you have created the evaluation criteria and evaluated the alternatives, the decision should be all but made for you. Remember, however, that after all of your calculations and analysis, you will have to make the decision based on your judgement of the situation. You will have to decide whether one factor is more important than another, and will choose to value some things above others.

Understanding emotions

There is evidence to suggest that you cannot make decisions without also making emotional choices such as these value judgements. Decision-making is not wholly rational, so be very careful about taking a decision that you are not entirely comfortable with. Your emotions or your subconcious may be telling you something important that the "rational" analysis has missed.

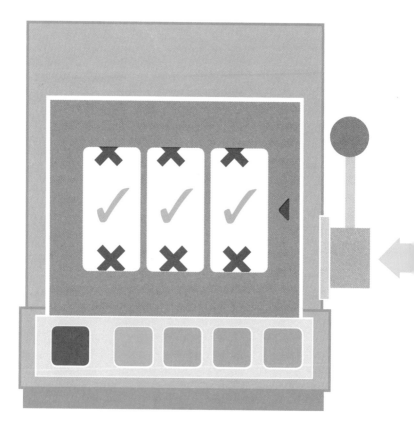

In focus

DEALING WITH RISK

All decisions contain risks. To assess the riskiness of your alternatives, ask:
• What is the best outcome I can contemplate?
• What is the most likely outcome?
• What is the worst outcome I can contemplate?

You can then estimate the probability of each outcome occurring and calculate the likely cost using a decision-tree diagram (see p.63). However, regardless of the outcome of these calculations there are two further questions you need to ask:
• Can the project survive if the worst-case scenario happens?
• Am I prepared to risk that probability of failure?

Your choice may depend on your appetite for risk. Others may have a different view, so ensure everyone understands the risks involved.

You will have to **decide** whether one factor is more **important** than another

Acting on your choice

Once the decision is made, you will need to communicate it to those who have been involved in the process as well as to those it will affect. Draw up an implementation plan and delegate authority to individuals who will be held responsible for implementing the decision. Appoint a project manager and a project sponsor to oversee the whole project where appropriate.

Evaluating the project

Once the project or task has been completed, evaluate how it went. This isn't a witch-hunt, but an opportunity to learn. Some of the best-performing companies regularly re-evaluate their projects to gain insight and learning for the future. You can even improve your personal decision-making ability by reflecting on what went well and what did not.

Saying "no"

Successful people know what they want and how they are going to get it, and say "no" when what they are being asked to do doesn't fit in with their plans. Being successful is as much about what you decide not to do as what you decide to do.

Tip

STRIKE A BALANCE
Fight the urge to work long hours to try **to impress** your bosses. For a senior position, employers prefer a **well-rounded individual** to a workaholic.

Maintaining a balance

We all have to keep a balance in our lives. You have to balance what your employer wants from you with what you get from your employer. The latter doesn't only mean money, but also the training you receive, the experience you get, and the opportunities that working for the company opens up for your career.

Assessing work time

You also have to balance your working life and your family life. If you want to get ahead, the company you work for will expect some commitment and flexibility, but you do not have to be a doormat. Decide how much time you are willing to give to the company and how much you will keep for your family, and then stick to it consistently. There will be times when intensive effort is required and you may have to put in long hours, but if your employer doesn't reciprocate, you should consider your position.

Decide how much **time** you are willing to give to the **company** and how much you will **keep** for your **family**, and then **stick to it**

ASK YOURSELF...
What's in it for me?   **YES** **NO**

1 Am I doing this because **I have to,** rather than because I want to? ☐ ☐

2 If I have to do it, will **I get something** in return? .... ☐ ☐

3 If I have to do it, can I make the task **more enjoyable,**
or develop the task to align more with my goals? .... ☐ ☐

4 If I have to do it, will I receive **recognition?** .... ☐ ☐

5 If I do this, will it help me **achieve my goals**
and ambitions? .... ☐ ☐

6 If I do this, will it give me **an experience** that can go
on my CV? .... ☐ ☐

7 If I do it, can I **maximize the benefit?** .... ☐ ☐

8 If I say no, will there be **consequences?** .... ☐ ☐

Getting it right
Use your judgement to assess when and how often you say no. It doesn't look good if you are seen as someone who always says no, or who only says no to the difficult jobs, so make sure that you get the balance right. When saying no is appropriate, do so quickly and politely.

Evaluating the project
You may sometimes find yourself in the situation where colleagues try to offload work on to you because they don't want to do it themselves, and they see you as being accommodating enough to do their work for them. If this happens, think very carefully before you accept. Assess the situation: if there really is a crisis and you can help, then of course you should do so. However, if there are no good

reasons and you feel the other person may make a habit of offloading their work, you should say no. Do this politely but firmly. Do not make complicated excuses, just say something like: "I'm sorry, but I can't help out this time. I have a heavy workload myself."

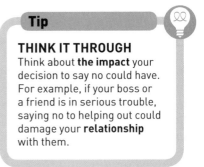

Tip

THINK IT THROUGH
Think about **the impact** your decision to say no could have. For example, if your boss or a friend is in serious trouble, saying no to helping out could damage your **relationship** with them.

Communicating successfully

Communication is about sharing and receiving information through a variety of channels, from formal presentation to general conversation, emails, reports, and letters. How you communicate, and the channel you use, say something about you – so take care.

Knowing your audience

The first lesson in effective communication is to think about your audience – the people with whom you are having a conversation, or who are reading your email or report, or listening on the other end of the telephone. Communication is a two-way process and your job is to make it easy for them to understand and focus on what you are saying or writing. Think about their level of knowledge of the subject, whether they are likely to understand technical terms or jargon you may be using. What is their particular interest in what you have to say and what outcomes do you hope to achieve?

61%
of **employers** claimed that a **spelling mistake** would make them instantly reject **an application** from a **candidate** for a job

COMPOSING AN EMAIL

Dos	Don'ts
O **Keeping it concise but clear**	O Using sloppy grammar
O **Keeping it short, but not abrupt**	O Using too many abbreviations
O **Putting key information in attachments, not in the main body of the email**	O Including so much detail that the email runs for several pages
O **Reading your email carefully before pressing "send"**	O Copying in others without thinking about the implications

Choosing the right communication channel

CHANNEL	ADVANTAGES	DISADVANTAGES
Telephone Best used for delivering good news or testing out an idea quickly	O You get an **immediate** response to your message O You can **test the reaction** of the other person O Personal, so helps **build a relationship**	O No written record of your **discussions** O You may **be calling** at the wrong time, and may get an ill-considered response
Meeting Best used for influencing people and for important or sensitive matters	O **Personal contact** helps to **build relationships** O You will be able to **gauge** reactions by reading the **body language** of the other person	O Setting up and attending **meetings** takes time O The person's **response** to a negative message may be difficult to handle
Letter Best used for lengthy and detailed information	O Provides a written **record** so may avoid disputes O As fewer letters are sent now, it makes your message **stand out**	O Your message will take time to **arrive** O You will not know if it has been **read** O You cannot see the **reaction** of the recipient
Email Best used for quick, short messages and urgent communication	O **Instant delivery** of your message O **Quick** to compose and to **send** O You can get a **quick response**	O You cannot see the **reaction** of the recipient O The message "tone" may be misinterpreted O May have had insufficient **thought**
Report Best used for proposals and to make arguments with evidence	O The **formal** structure **helps** in constructing arguments and presenting evidence O You can detail your **thoughts and rationale**	O **Takes time** to compile and write O If it is too long, it may not be read **thoroughly**

Shaping the content

Whether you are composing an email, writing a letter, or just speaking to someone on the telephone, you should prepare what you are going to say and how you say it. For something relatively simple, this may just mean organizing your thoughts and thinking about the best way to express them. For a more complicated or sensitive matter it may be useful to jot down your ideas on a piece of paper and see how they link together; this should help you to structure your message.

Always read what you have written in an email or letter, to check that it means what you want to say. For every message you write, ask yourself:
- Will my readers understand this?
- Have I captured their interest?
- Does this mean what I want it to mean, and have I got the tone right?
- Will this achieve the aim I want?
- Have I structured my thoughts in a logical way?
- Is it well laid out, concise, and jargon-free, and are the spelling and grammar correct?

Getting your message right

HIT THE RIGHT LEVEL

Adjust your level of formality to match the individual person, the organization, or the culture of the company or person you are communicating with at the time.

If you have to **present facts and figures,** remember that **visuals** are often much **clearer than words**

Writing reports

A report is normally designed to present facts, figures, and recommendations for action. The structure, tone, and length will depend on the purpose. A report on a serious accident, for example, which may have legal ramifications, will have to be more thorough and detailed than, say, a recommendation to buy a particular model of printer.

All the essential elements of good communication apply to the writing of a report. Keep it concise, without losing meaning, make it understandable and interesting to the reader, and make sure it reflects what you want to say. If you have to present facts and figures, remember that visuals are often much clearer than words.

> Always **read what you have written** in an email or letter, to **check** that it means what **you want to say**

KEEP IT SIMPLE

Use short words and uncomplicated sentence construction to aid comprehension – sending a clear message will give the reader a good impression of you.

BE CONCISE

Don't use unnecessary words – they will dilute your message and may confuse the reader. Use "when...", for example, rather than "at a time when...".

HIGHLIGHT KEY POINTS

Use bullet points to help isolate important points for emphasis, but avoid using too many or they will lose their impact.

CHECK YOUR PUNCTUATION

Clear punctuation helps your reader understand what you have written, and is key to delivering a precise message.

BE DIRECT

Use the active rather than the passive voice to deliver your message. For example, say: "Mr. Skoog took the machine away" rather than "The machine was taken away by Mr. Skoog."

Listening effectively

Many people can talk, but few listen well. If you are good at hearing what others miss, it gives you a distinct advantage. Good listeners are also better at building rapport with others, so listening effectively is a good skill to develop and practise.

Being a good listener

Listening is not the same as hearing. You can hear something but not take it in or respond to it. The words are just flowing over you. When you are truly listening, the person talking to you knows you are listening and will appreciate it. Listening requires concentration, which will not be possible if you are busy thinking about what you are going to say next. Be in the present. If you are really listening you will find your next words come intuitively.

Reading all signs

Listen to what the speaker is saying, not just what you are hearing. Think about what the tone and inflection in the voice tells you about what's behind the words. Are they congruent? If not, what is not being said? Their body language is important, too, and you will probably pick this up subconsciously. Does the speaker's body language match their words?

Confirming your thoughts

As you listen, make sure that you always understand what the speaker is saying. Summarize your understanding and, if necessary, ask the speaker to repeat what he or she said, or ask for further clarification if you are unsure. Never pretend to understand if you don't.

Ending well

Finally, make sure that you end the encounter on the right note. If you need to take further action as a result of your conversation, summarize what you have heard and then discuss the action you are going to take. Make a note of what you have agreed should happen next, ideally in your colleagues' presence. This will emphasize the importance of the matters that have been discussed and decided. Always make a note of important points even if this has to be after the meeting.

Tip

GIVE THE RIGHT SIGNS
Give **signs of encouragement** – nods, smiles, and winces in the right places – to the person you are **listening** to. If the story is distressing or embarrassing, it is better to **vary your eye contact**.

Giving advice

There will be times when you get the impression that a conversation is actually a request for advice. Be wary of this. It's better to be asked for advice than to offer it unsolicited. If you really feel you have something important to contribute, ask the person whether your advice is welcome, but be prepared to be told "no". Alternatively, give advice by telling a personal story of how you dealt with something similar. Do this carefully, however – no two circumstances are identical.

Empathizing with care

There are some times when there is nothing you can do. The person may be telling you something simply to tell someone. In this case, your role is to listen carefully and empathize, letting him or her know you are always available if you are needed. Above all, when someone tells you something in confidence, keep that confidence.

When you are **truly listening**, the person **talking** to you will realise and **appreciate it**

CHECKLIST...
Listening well

	YES	NO
Think about the last real conversation you had:		
1 Was I really **listening** to what was being said?	☐	☐
2 Were **my responses** appropriate while the speaker was talking?	☐	☐
3 Did my actions **encourage** or interrupt the flow?	☐	☐
4 Were my questions **well crafted** and appropriate?	☐	☐
5 Did I close the **discussion** appropriately?	☐	☐
6 Was I **helpful**?	☐	☐

Becoming
successful

To achieve success in your professional life you need to bring together a coherent set of higher-level skills, from leadership and management to networking and personal development. Regularly monitoring and steering your progress, whether alone or with the help of an experienced mentor, is an integral part of the process.

04

Moving into leadership

A leader has the personal characteristics that make people want to follow them, the ability to create and communicate a purpose, and the personal touch to deal with people. To be a leader, you must want to become a leader and be committed to learning and practising leadership skills.

Making a great leader

To be a great leader, you do not necessarily have to be a good organizer, but you must ensure that work is capably organized and managed. You don't have to be a great strategist, but you must ensure that strategy is developed, delivered, and communicated. You don't have to be a brilliant decision-maker, but you must ensure that tough decisions are taken at the right time and implemented sympathetically. The first lesson of effective leadership, therefore, is that you must surround yourself with good people with the right skills, whom you can trust to deliver.

> Surround yourself with **good people** with the right skills

Defining leadership

While it is true to say that leaders are made, not born, they tend to share certain characteristics. They have integrity, displaying standards and values that make people trust them. They show enthusiasm, and can create it in others. They tend to have a warm personality and interact well with others and they are tough but fair, with high standards and expectations, but always dealing with people fairly and openly.

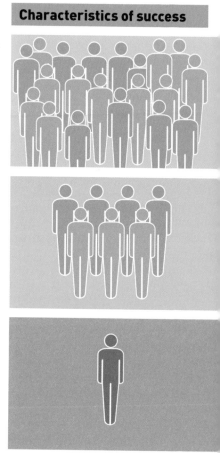

Characteristics of success

Aiming for the top

When you become a leader you will usually have three main aims, which often overlap and sometimes conflict with one another:

- To create a vision for the organization
- To ensure team cohesiveness to deliver the vision
- To satisfy the needs of the individuals within the team.

Juggling these balls is your task: if you drop any one, the organization or team is likely to stumble. Teams and individuals do not work well without a purpose or goal to achieve. This is because most individuals find it hard to achieve goals if they do not work as a team; and teams usually fail to achieve their goals without motivated individuals.

HIGH-PERFORMING ORGANIZATIONS

- O Are **very clear** about where they want to be and the measures of success
- O Know where they have come from and **respect their past**
- O **Understand** where they are now and where they stand against their competitors

HIGH-PERFORMING TEAMS

- O Have clear and **realistic objectives**
- O Share a **sense of purpose**
- O Create an **open atmosphere**
- O Regularly and objectively **review progress**
- O Build on their **experiences**
- O **Work through** difficult times together

HIGH-PERFORMING PEOPLE

- O Feel **valued and respected**
- O **Know** what is required of them at work
- O Have the **tools and resources** to do their jobs well
- O Know how what they do **helps** the organization to be **successful**
- O Are **nurtured and developed**

Succeeding as a manager

The role of the manager is to implement the organization's strategy through his or her stewardship of the available resources. Just like the leadership role, there are conflicts and tensions that have to be resolved, and all managers need to be leaders to some extent.

Defining the role

As a manager, your focus is on the delivery of tasks, on the efficient use and coordination of resources, and on developing capabilities of people within your team or organization. You must quickly realize that you cannot do everything yourself, and develop skills in setting objectives for yourself and for others, in delegating tasks, and in managing your team.

| 01

Communicate the big picture. What is the organization trying to achieve and how does your team fit in?

> **Develop skills** in **setting objectives** for yourself and for others, in **delegating** tasks, and in **managing** your **team**

Delegating tasks

Delegation is about giving responsibility to others for part of a project, so freeing time for you to co-ordinate the work of all members of the team, like the conductor of an orchestra. It's also a good way of developing people – of growing their skills, experience, and confidence. You need to be clear in communicating the tasks to be delegated, the standards and goals to be achieved, and the boundaries of what can and can't be done. Not all tasks are suitable for delegation. Don't delegate unless the objectives of a task are:

- Clear, specific, and measureable
- Targeted and achievable in a set time
- Worthwhile and realistic, but also challenging
- Written and recorded
- Consistent with the goals of the organization
- Set participatively

Managing team performance

03
Discuss, as a team, how these will be achieved and develop an outline plan.

04
Decide how the tasks in the plan will be distributed among the team, the milestones to be achieved, and who will be responsible for what.

05
Delegate tasks to team members. Avoid telling people in detail how the task is to be performed – leave them to get on with it.

02
Explain the objectives you have to achieve and the measures on which you will be judged.

06
Meet individual members on a one-to-one basis at regular intervals. Monitor progress, listen to their needs and concerns, and provide support.

07
Meet as a team regularly to review progress, track the performance measures, reallocate resources as necessary, and revise the plan when needed.

08
Share the team's success and accept personal responsibility for failure.

Networking

Networking is about establishing groups of contacts that will add value to your business and career. It is a two-way process in which you must give to receive. Building good relationships will give you a competitive edge, but for many people, the thought of going out to make contacts is awkward and artificial.

Six degrees of separation

Research carried out by the American social psychologist Stanley Milgram suggested that most people are connected to one another through a chain of just six acquaintances. Networking gives you access to a wealth of knowledge and expertise; it allows you to gain competitive information, build a good reputation, and even get your next job. And as you progress in your career, who you know becomes increasingly, and sometimes critically, important.

78% of people **online** could connect with each other via **six linked messages**

Valuing networks

Networking is about building relationships, not selling. Your network should include not just customers, but others in your profession or trade with whom you can share experience, as well as suppliers, consultants, and others with influence. Do not forget about internal networks, which may be as important as external contacts in large organizations.

Meeting people

You can meet people anywhere. Be open to chance contacts, at airports or in elevators for example; these unexpected opportunities to meet people and network can prove invaluable. Business contacts are increasingly made online, through targeted research or in business networking groups, but there is still no substitute for old-fashioned, face-to-face networking.

Tip

TARGET YOUR NETWORKING

Make a "hit list" of people you **want to meet**; keep your eyes and ears **open for opportunities**.

Choosing an event

Conferences are excellent arenas for networking, because they bring together a group of individuals who have a variety of interests in a common subject. At a conference on corporate responsibility, for example, you are likely to meet people from other organizations who are in a similar position to you, as well as experts in various aspects of the subject. You may make contacts with suppliers of equipment that could reduce your company's environmental impact, or consultants who could provide advice.

Working a conference

Try not to take too much with you to a conference. If you're loaded with bags, files, a laptop, and stacks of sales brochures, it's hard to appear cool and collected.

In focus

INTRODUCTIONS

At conferences, make an effort to introduce your contacts to other people. The generally accepted rule is to introduce the junior person to the more senior. So, introduce a colleague to a customer or a manager to a director. Try to say something about the person you are introducing that will provide a starting point for conversation. For example: "Leo, I'd like to introduce Annabelle, who worked on our corporate responsibility programme." Don't hesitate to ask someone to introduce you to one of their contacts if it's difficult for you to do so yourself.

CHECKLIST...
Preparing for meetings

	YES	NO
1 Have I **studied** the attendance list and marked people I want to meet?	☐	☐
2 Have I **researched** those people beforehand?	☐	☐
3 Is there anyone I **know already** on the list?	☐	☐
4 Do I know what the **dress code** is?	☐	☐
5 Do I have my **business cards** with me?	☐	☐

It can be daunting to walk into a room full of people, but there are ways to appear composed. Smile as you walk in and look for any existing acquaintances. Talking to people you know first can help ease you in, but don't stay with them for more than a few minutes.

Introducing yourself
If you don't know anyone, join a group of two or three people who don't appear too engrossed in conversation. Smile, and say something like, "Hello, I hope I'm not interrupting your conversation. I'm ....". Give your name and company. In almost all cases they will smile back and invite you to join them.

Where possible, try to enlarge the group you're talking with. This enables you to meet more people and makes it easier for you to move on when it is appropriate. Do this by noting any people standing nearby, and turning towards them when you speak. By addressing your comments to them as well as the group, you will bring them into the conversation.

Connecting with delegates
Be attentive to the people in your group, don't scan the room beyond for other prospects – this makes it impossible to create rapport. Ask open questions that will reveal common ground, and be sure to give other people in your group an opportunity to speak.

Exit your conversations politely. If you want to keep in touch, make sure that you exchange business cards. There are rules about giving and receiving business cards in some countries, however, so do your research before attending international gatherings.

Tip

BE SELECTIVE
It may be hard to imagine now, but with practice, you may well come to **enjoy networking**. Be methodical, and attend only the events where you need to be seen or are **likely to meet the people** you want to meet.

Recording your contacts

Networking time will be wasted if you do not record and follow up your contacts. Your record can be very simple – a note of name, company, and contact details, the context of the meeting, a brief account of what was said, and a summary of what you think this person could do for you, or vice versa. Some people find it useful to group their contacts as:

DECISION-MAKERS:
people who can award contracts

INFLUENCERS:
people whose opinions usually carry weight

Developing your network

There are software packages that can help you record and manage your contacts, but check the legal data protection requirements in your country before compiling information digitally.

Your network list needs nurturing and maintenance; people will fall off without regular contact. Review your list periodically and identify conspicuous gaps. Remember that when people leave a company they remain as your contacts, so keep in touch – they may go on to bigger and better things and become even more useful to you.

How to follow up contacts

93%

of **marketing** professionals use **social media** networks for their **business**

Always send a thank-you email or letter after every meeting you have attended.

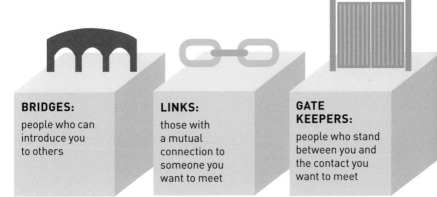

BRIDGES:
people who can introduce you to others

LINKS:
those with a mutual connection to someone you want to meet

GATE KEEPERS:
people who stand between you and the contact you want to meet

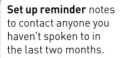

Set up reminder notes to contact anyone you haven't spoken to in the last two months.

Arrange to meet only if you have a real purpose for a meeting, otherwise email or post a snippet of useful information.

Bring some new ideas with you to the meeting to stimulate thinking.

If you do want a meeting, make sure the other person knows why, and clarify time limits for the meeting.

Working with a mentor

Finding and using a good mentor can be highly beneficial both to your career and to your personal well-being. A good mentor is impartial, has more experience than you in key areas, and acts as a safe and effective sounding board for your ideas.

Defining the role

Mentors are people who guide others through periods of change towards agreed objectives. They can help you in a number of ways. First, they can enable you to work through your problems in a safe environment. They may not solve your problems for you (you need to learn to do so), but they will ask questions to make you analyze your position and alert you to pitfalls or alternatives. Second, they can give advice. This may be in the form of what to do, or who to approach within the organization to obtain help. They may point you towards training and development programmes, or suggest projects that you should consider being involved with.

Third, they may open up your career. They may have access to interesting job opportunities before they become widely available and may suggest roles that you would never have considered. If they are external to your company, they may have their own networks of contacts, but don't expect this as part of the relationship.

Choosing a mentor

Your organization may run a mentoring service, but if they do not, you will have to set up a more informal mentoring relationship. The person you select as your mentor must, of course, possess the experience you want to access and should also be someone with whom you can build a good working relationship. He or she may not be a technical expert in the field in which you are working. This can be a real advantage because it enables you to work through issues from a fresh perspective.

77%

of **companies** in one survey claimed that their **mentoring programmes** helped to **increase** their **employee retention**

ASK YOURSELF...
What type of mentor do I need? **YES NO**

1 Have I decided if I need someone who is **internal or external** to my current organization? .... ☐ ☐

2 Is there a **specific issue** I really want help with?........................... ☐ ☐

3 Is this a **short-term need,** not a long-term relationship? .... ☐ ☐

4 Is there an **area of expertise** my mentor should have (psychology, leadership, career guidance)?................................... ☐ ☐

Qualities of a good mentor

The attributes of a good mentor depend on your circumstances and on your specific role, but he or she should always be:

- Someone you respect and trust, and who won't always just agree with what you say
- Someone you consider to be a role model
- Someone who listens, probing what you say in order to understand you
- Someone who is genuinely interested in you and what you want to do, and who is available when you need help.

Mentoring in-house

Mentors are typically separate from the line-management relationship, but your boss may be the ideal candidate, especially when the difference in age and seniority is large. Some companies establish roles where this is designed to happen – Assistant to the Managing Director, for example.

If you have a very senior manager or director as your mentor, it can open doors to people whom you would not normally meet. Also, it may give you insights into the organization's political process, identify career opportunities, and protect you when things go wrong.

Tip

THINK BEFORE YOU SPEAK
Remember that your boss is part of the organization, so if he or she is your mentor, be cautious about being **completely open** about every aspect of your **ambitions** or personal life.

Moving on

For some, the ideal career is a series of well-timed promotions within one organization, but gaining job satisfaction often necessitates finding a new role in a new company. Each move you make should give you the experience to progress in your career, so you should choose youropportunities carefully. But when is the right time to change and when is it better to stay put?

Achieving promotion

Getting promoted within your organization depends on being seen to be doing a good job and having the capability of doing a bigger job. You will probably need to improve your visibility within the company and cultivate key internal contacts, so become known more widely. Try putting yourself forward as a spokesperson for your team, or devise presentations on aspects of your work that you can deliver to a wider audience. Many large organizations run fast-track schemes, so make sure both your boss and the Human Resources department know you are interested.

Considering options

A job is not just its title – it is the experience you gain and what you will be able to make of this experience in your later career. If you are in a clerical role, for example, why not volunteer to be involved in the continuous improvement programme. And if people don't see you as management material, volunteer for an external role, perhaps with a charity, and develop your leadership skills that way. Talk to your boss about opportunities that may be open to you. If you are a valued employee, your organization will be interested in your future.

Changing jobs

You may need to leave your current organization to achieve your aims, but don't act without careful consideration. Ask yourself where you want to go to next, rather than focusing on escaping from the present. How will your move look on your CV three or five years from now? Future employers usually look favourably on an internal promotion on your CV. Above all, try very hard never to leave a job on a sour note – you will probably need an excellent reference or testimonial from your current employer to get your next job.

Seeking opportunity

Prospective employers are looking for evidence of five attributes:

01 Appropriate **qualifications**

02 A relevant range of **experience**

03 **Specific skills** required for the post

04 **Previous positions** held

05 How **successful** you have been

At the interview stage employers will also **assess** your **attitude and "fit"** with the organization. Examine any job advert and try to decode it in the context of these attributes.

CHECKLIST...
Deciding if it is time to leave a job

	YES	NO
1 Have I already **gained** all the **experience** I can get from my current role?...	☐	☐
2 Have I exhausted all the **development opportunities** open to me?	☐	☐
3 Do I have the appetite for **a change?**	☐	☐
4 Am I in **good health?**	☐	☐
5 Is the new job really **a promotion?**..................................	☐	☐
6 Will the new job provide the **experience and opportunities** I need for my future?..............................	☐	☐

Getting that job

When seeking your next position, make sure that you consider and address each of the five qualities that recruiters are looking for in your application.

Experience is what you gain from **each job** and **each project** you undertake

Key points for successful job applications

01 **Qualifications** These give an indication of your potential and so are particularly important in more junior jobs. Even working towards a qualification signals commitment and ambition to your current, or future, employer. Examine job adverts in your area of expertise and analyze what qualifications employers are seeking; if you don't have them, enrol on a suitable course.

02 **Experience** There is no substitute for experience, but employers are not necessarily looking for candidates who have spent long periods in the same role – two or three years is often adequate. If you have spent less time in a role, and particularly if you have moved several times, you may be seen as someone who lacks commitment. If you have held one job for much longer, you may be perceived to be too set in your ways.

Experience is what you gain from each job and each project you undertake. If you make a mistake, learn from it. Reflect on everything you have done and what you have learnt. Also, use someone to help you through a project so you can learn in real time. A mentor (see pp.86–87), a good colleague, or even a family member can sometimes fulfil this role.

03 **Skills** Many of the basic skills you will need in any job, such as negotiating, presenting, managing your time, and chairing meetings, have been covered in this book. To hone your skills, identify your preferred learning style and choose development experiences that best suit you:

- Do you learn best from reading books, trade magazines, or online training material?
- Do you prefer learning in the classroom, at conferences, or from colleagues? Short courses give you the opportunity to develop specific skills away from your colleagues, in a safe environment.
- Do you learn best by doing the task? A great way to learn something is by teaching it to someone else.

04 **Position** Grand job titles will look good on your CV and may get you shortlisted for interview, but they are no substitute for experience. Discrepancies are sure to come to light when you are interviewed by your new employer, so be realistic.

When you apply for a new job, check that the content of the advertised role matches the title. Is it really going to offer you the experience you want? For example, the title of Assistant General Manager may sound great, but in reality, will you be deputizing for the General Manager or will you be little more than a clerical assistant?

05 **Success** Most recruiters are looking for success and may not even shortlist you for interview if they don't see evidence of progression on your CV. More astute recruiters will want to examine how you have dealt with difficult and challenging situations. They want to see if you are someone who learns. To address this requirement, present yourself through a success story about your past. For example, compare the two statements below:

- "I was financial controller of a division in Cape Town for three years and every month the books were closed on time."
- "I led a project to replace the accounting system with new software: it was delivered on time and in budget."
- The second statement clearly conveys success, where the first simply describes a role. Showing that you have taken up development opportunities and have been successful makes your CV stand out from the crowd.

TAKING YOUR CAREER FORWARD

Dos	Don'ts
O **Working towards qualifications you will need in the future**	O Focusing only on improving your technical skills
O **Demonstrating progression from junior roles to positions of responsibility**	O Expecting to be promoted purely on your impressive qualifications
O **Seeking out new experiences, and actively learning from them**	O Leaving responsibility for your development to your employer
O **Using a mentor to help with your personal development**	O Resenting your lack of promotion

Reviewing your plans

Planning your personal and professional development is essential to achieving high performance, but plans have a habit of being overtaken by events. New opportunities will arise and circumstances change, making it vital to review your progress.

Navigating your success

HOW DO I LOOK TO MY EMPLOYER?
Does my employer:

O **think** I am helpful?

O **value** my contribution?

O **think** I am promotable?

O **trust** and respect me?

O **use** me in projects beyond my role?

Monitoring your progress

At least once a year, you should review your progress against your development plan. Ask yourself questions such as:

- Have I attained the goals I set myself in my plan? If not, why?
- Are my goals unattainable or are they just going to take a bit longer?
- What have I achieved that wasn't in my plan? What new opportunities does this give me?

Reviewing the plan

Review the development plan to see if it still reflects what you want to do with your personal and professional life. Think about whether your development has made your plan unfeasible, whether new opportunities have arisen, or whether your objectives have changed. Do you need to modify your plan or create a new one from scratch?

Development encompasses more than your position and progress at work. Successful people tend to be well rounded, with a variety of interests and experience, and they measure their success in terms other than how much money they have made and the status they have. Assess and review your own development by asking yourself questions about your current level of success – for example, how well you perform and are developing and learning, how you benefit from work, and how you look to your employer.

Review your own **development** by asking questions about your **current success**

HOW DO I BENEFIT FROM WORK?
Am I satisfied with:

- O **my level** of pay?
- O **the benefits** I receive?
- O **my work–life** balance?
- O **the opportunities** this job gives me?
- O **my current** role?

HOW AM I DEVELOPING?
Have I:

- O **met** the development targets I have set myself?
- O **kept** my skills up to date?
- O **learnt** something new at work this week?
- O **reviewed** my development plan in the last six months?

HOW WELL DO I PERFORM?
Do I:

- O **work** in a team that achieves work objectives and targets?
- O **consistently** meet my own work objectives and targets?
- O **support** my colleagues?
- O **have** the experience and skills and the support and tools to do my job well?

Index

Acknowledgments

Authors' acknowledgments

We would like to acknowledge and thank Mike's friends and colleagues at the Centre for Business Performance, Cranfield School of Management for their support and ideas incorporated into this book. We would also like to thank the Institute of Chartered Accountants in England and Wales for giving Pippa the time to write this book and in particular Charles Carter and Debbie Kimpton for their support.

Publisher's acknowledgments

The publisher would like to thank Hilary Bird and Margaret McCormack for indexing, Judy Barratt for proofreading, Phil Gamble for design assistance, and Charles Wills for co-ordinating Americanization.

Original edition:
Senior Editor Peter Jones
Senior Art Editor Helen Spencer
Production Editor Ben Marcus
Production Controller Hema Gohil
Executive Managing Editor
    Adèle Hayward
Managing Art Editor Kat Mead
Art Director Peter Luff
Publisher Stephanie Jackson

First edition produced for Dorling Kindersley Limited by Cobalt id
www.cobaltid.co.uk

Editors
Kati Dye, Maddy King, Marek Walisiewicz